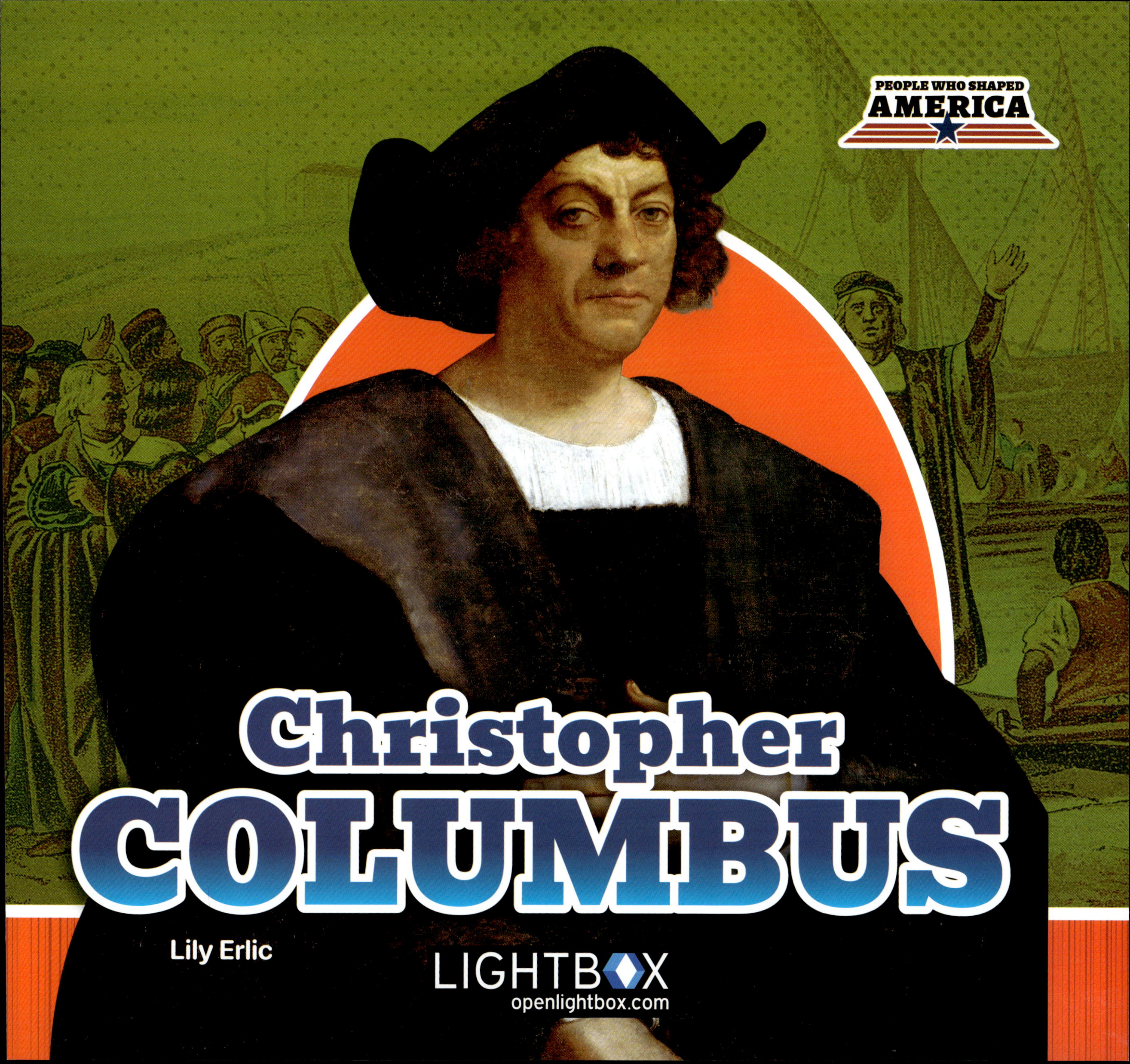

PEOPLE WHO SHAPED AMERICA

# Christopher COLUMBUS

Lily Erlic

LIGHTBOX
openlightbox.com

# LIGHTBOX

Go to **www.openlightbox.com** and enter this book's unique code.

**ACCESS CODE**

**LBXZ2429**

Lightbox is an all-inclusive digital solution for the teaching and learning of curriculum topics in an original, groundbreaking way.

**OPTIMIZED FOR**

- ✓ TABLETS
- ✓ SMART BOARDS
- ✓ COMPUTERS
- ✓ AND MUCH MORE!

## STANDARD FEATURES OF LIGHTBOX

- **AUDIO** High-quality narration using text-to-speech system
- **VIDEOS** Embedded high-definition video clips
- **ACTIVITIES** Printable PDFs that can be emailed and graded
- **WEBLINKS** Curated links to external, child-safe resources
- **SLIDESHOWS** Pictorial overviews of key concepts
- **INTERACTIVE MAPS** Interactive maps and aerial satellite imagery
- **QUIZZES** Ten multiple choice questions that are automatically graded and emailed for teacher assessment
- **KEY WORDS** Matching key concepts to their definitions

## SUPPLEMENTARY RESOURCES

- **SHARE** Share titles within your Learning Management System (LMS) or Library Circulation System
- **CURRICULUM** Find national and state curriculum correlations
- **CITATION** Create bibliographical references following APA, CMSO, and MLA styles

**VIDEOS**

**WEBLINKS**

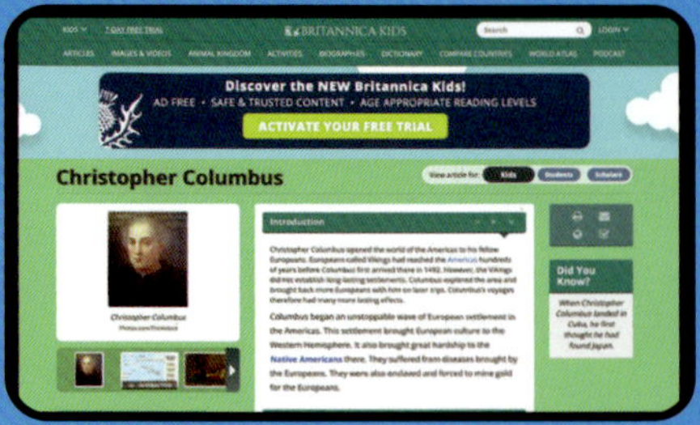


**SLIDESHOWS**

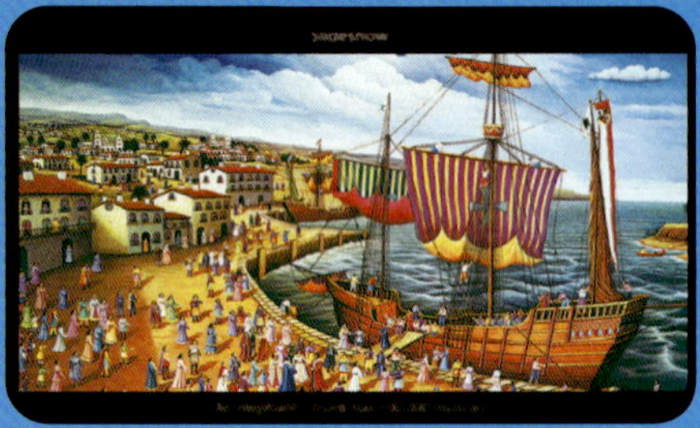

**QUIZZES**

**This title is part of our Lightbox digital subscription**

**1-Year Texas Subscription**
978-1-5105-8659-8

Access hundreds of Lightbox titles with our digital subscription.
Sign up for a **FREE** subscription trial at **www.openlightbox.com/trial**

The digital components of this book are guaranteed to stay active for at least five years from the date of publication.

PEOPLE WHO SHAPED AMERICA

# Christopher COLUMBUS

## CONTENTS

# Who Was Christopher Columbus?

Christopher Columbus was an explorer. He hoped to find a new route from Europe to Asia. Instead, he sailed to the Americas.

Christopher **sailed** from **Spain** to the **Americas** in **1492**.

ARCTIC CIRCLE
ICELAND
1001
HUDSON'S STRAIT
Frobisher's Str.
NORWAY
SWEDEN
NORTH SEA
SCOTLAND
IRELAND
ENGLAND
ENGLISH CHANNEL
HOLLAND
BELGIUM
GERMANY
PRUSSIA
FRANCE
EUROPE
AUSTRIA
ITALY
BAY OF BISCAY
Cape Finisterre
PORTUGAL
SPAIN
MEDITERRANEAN SEA
Str. of Gibraltar
Azores
Quebec
Montreal
R. St. Lawrence
L. Ontario
NEW BRUNSWICK
Cape Cod
Delaware Bay
Chesapeake Bay
C. Hatteras

# Growing Up

Christopher was born in 1451. When he was young, he liked to study maps and go sailing. As a teenager, he worked on a ship.

**Christopher** was **born** in the city of **Genoa**, now part of **Italy**.

# Overcoming Obstacles

Christopher was sure there was a faster way to get to Asia. He asked the king and queen of Spain to help him find it.

They gave him money for ships and a crew.

# Values

Christopher was brave and daring. Sailing to faraway lands was dangerous. He did it anyway.

# Land in Sight

Christopher reached the Americas on October 12, 1492. Over time, many more people made the same journey.

Christopher had **three** ships **for his voyage**. They were the *Pinta*, *Niña,* and *Santa Maria*.

# Thoughts from Christopher

Christopher believed in taking risks. He was not afraid to try new things. He was open to adventure.

"I should not proceed by land to the East, as is custom, but by a Westerly route, in which direction we have hitherto no certain evidence that any one has gone."

– Christopher Columbus

# Explorer

Christopher sailed to the Americas four times. He explored many Caribbean islands. He also traveled to South America.

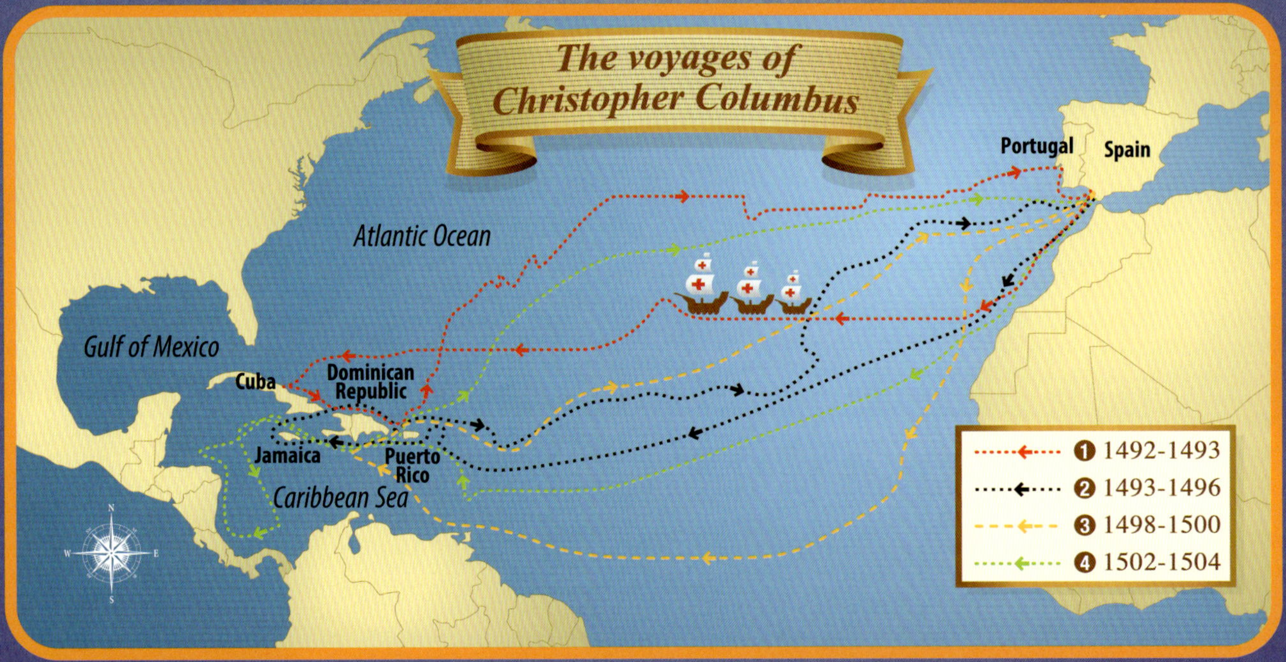

# Achievements and Successes

Christopher's voyages brought many people to the Americas. These people built towns and cities. Over time, new countries were formed.

**Columbus Day** was created in **1937**. It honors **Christopher's arrival** in the **New World**.

# Christopher Columbus Timeline

**1451**
Born

**1476**
Moves to Lisbon, Portugal

**1492**
Sails toward the Americas

**1493**
Second voyage to the New World

**1498**
Third voyage to the New World

**1502**
Shipwrecked in Jamaica on fourth voyage

**1506**
Dies in Spain at the age of 55

**2023**
A letter Christopher wrote about his first voyage sells for $3.9 million.

# Cause and Effect

## Cause

Christopher trained to be a sailor.

## Effect

He gained the experience needed to command his own ship.

## Cause

Christopher was a daring explorer.

## Effect

He sailed to the New World four times and visited many lands.

# KEY WORDS

Research has shown that as much as 65 percent of all written material published in English is made up of 300 words. These 300 words cannot be taught using pictures or learned by sounding them out. They must be recognized by sight. This book contains 69 common sight words to help young readers improve their reading fluency and comprehension. This book also teaches young readers several important content words, such as proper nouns. These words are paired with pictures to aid in learning and improve understanding.

| Page | Sight Words First Appearance |
|---|---|
| 4 | a, Americas, an, find, from, he, in, new, the, to, was, who |
| 7 | and, as, city, go, now, of, on, part, study, up, when, young |
| 8 | asked, for, get, help, him, it, there, they, way |
| 10 | did, lands |
| 12 | had, his, made, many, more, over, people, same, three, time, were |
| 15 | any, but, by, has, have, I, is, no, not, one, open, should, that, things, thoughts, try, we, which |
| 16 | also, four |
| 19 | day, these, world |

| Page | Content Words First Appearance |
|---|---|
| 4 | Asia, Christopher Columbus, Europe, explorer, route, Spain |
| 7 | Genoa, Italy, maps, sailing, ship, teenager |
| 8 | crew, king, money, obstacles, queen, ships |
| 11 | values |
| 12 | journey, *Niña*, *Pinta*, *Santa Maria*, sight, voyage |
| 15 | adventure, custom, direction, East, evidence, risks |
| 16 | Caribbean islands, South America |
| 19 | achievements, arrival, Columbus Day, countries, New World, successes, towns |

Published by Lightbox Learning Inc.
276 5th Avenue, Suite 704 #917
New York, NY 10001
Website: www.openlightbox.com



Library of Congress Control Number: 2024933865

ISBN 978-1-5105-8378-8 (hardcover)
ISBN 978-1-5105-8379-5 (static multi-user eBook)
ISBN 978-1-5105-8381-8 (interactive multi-user eBook)

Printed in Guangzhou, China
1 2 3 4 5 6 7 8 9 0 28 27 26 25 24

052024
110823

Project Coordinator: Heather Kissock
Designer: Jean Faye Rodriguez

Every reasonable effort has been made to trace ownership and to obtain permission to reprint copyright material. The publisher would be pleased to have any errors or omissions brought to its attention so that they may be corrected in subsequent printings.

The publisher acknowledges Getty Images, Alamy, Shutterstock, and Bridgeman Images as its primary image suppliers for this title.